DE:CODE

LEARN THE LANGUAGE OF

VIDEO GAMES

BY WILLIAM ANTHONY

BookLife
PUBLISHING

©2019
BookLife Publishing Ltd.
King's Lynn
Norfolk, PE30 4LS

All rights reserved.
Printed in Malaysia.

A catalogue record for this
book is available from the
British Library.

ISBN: 978-1-78637-692-3

Written by:
William Anthony

Edited by:
Madeline Tyler

Designed by:
Dan Scase

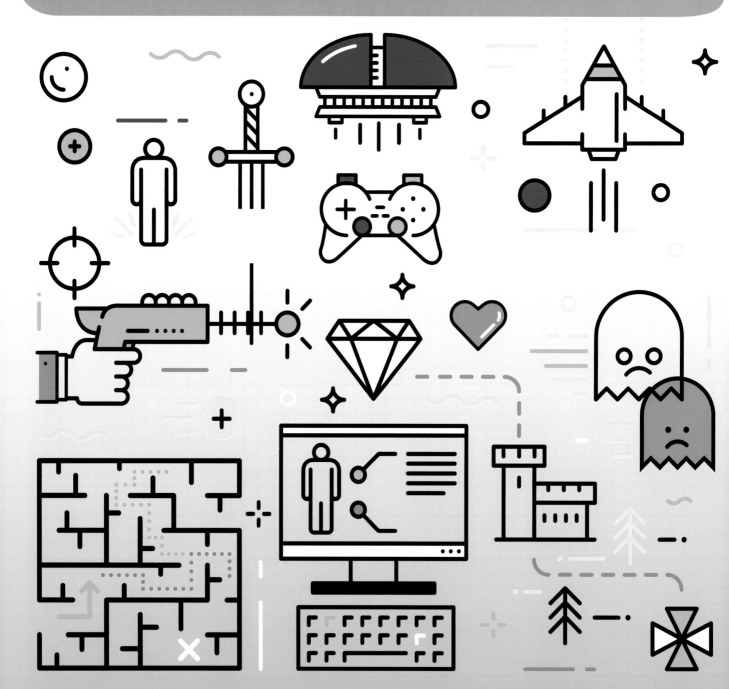

PHOTO CREDITS

HOW TO DE:CODE THE LANGUAGE OF VIDEO GAMES

There are lots of different weird and wonderful words in the world of video games. This handy guide will help you learn them all – but first, let's take a look at how to De:Code each word.

BETA
(BAY-TUH)
Noun: a version of a game that is nearly complete. It is open to a small number of users to find bugs or problems in the game before it is released. See **BUG**.

HEADWORD: this shows you how a word is spelt. These words are organised in alphabetical order.

PRONUNCIATION GUIDE: this tells you how to say a word out loud. Say each part exactly how it's written to pronounce the word correctly.

Word class: this is the type of word that the headword is. In this book you will see some of these:
- Noun – a person, place or thing
- Verb – an action word
- Adjective – a describing word

Abbreviations: this is the type of word that the headword is. In this book you will see some of these:
- Initialism – a set of letters taken from several words that are read as individual letters
- Acronym – a set of letters taken from several words that make a new word

Definition: this is what the headword means.

RELATED WORDS: this shows you other words that link to the one you're looking at.

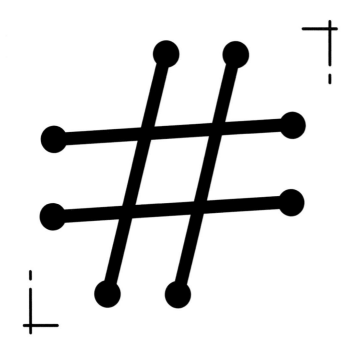

4K

Adjective: used to describe technology or content that provides a very sharp on-screen image.

It is around four times the quality of a HD image.

2D GAME

Noun: a game that appears flat on the screen, with no depth in the design. These make good platform games.

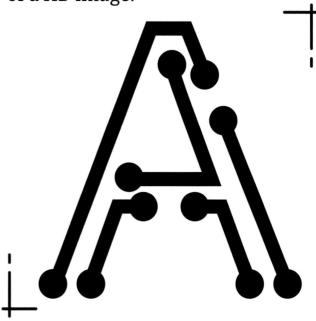

3D GAME

Noun: a game that resembles real life, in that it has depth in its design and does not appear flat on the screen.

ABANDONWARE

Noun: a game that has been forgotten about or put on hold by its developers. These games may end up getting cancelled altogether. See **VAPORWARE**.

ACCELEROMETER
(AX-SELL-UH-ROM-EH-TUR)

Noun: a device built into a controller that measures the movement of the player holding it. See **CONTROLLER**.

ACHIEVEMENT
(UH-CHEEV-MENT)
Noun: something that is unlocked when the player completes a specific event or challenge in a game. Slang terms: cheevo, cheevs.

AMMO
Noun: short for ammunition, the amount of equipment you have that can be used with or without a weapon to defeat enemies.

AVATAR
(AH-VUH-TAR)
Noun: an image or symbol that represents a person on their account.

ACTION-ADVENTURE GAME
Noun: a type of game where the player can explore the game-world as well as take part in live combat.

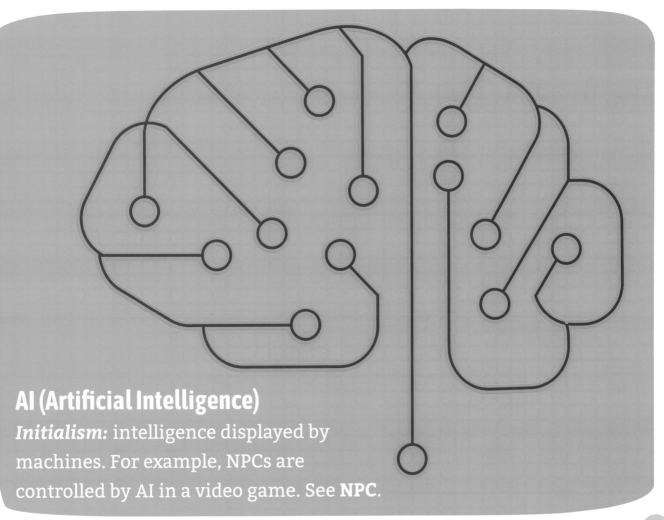

AI (Artificial Intelligence)
Initialism: intelligence displayed by machines. For example, NPCs are controlled by AI in a video game. See **NPC**.

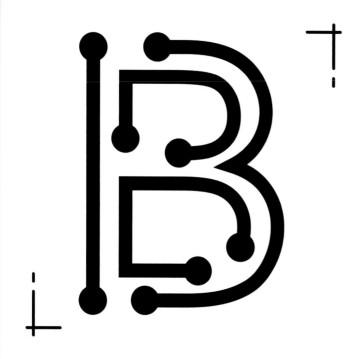

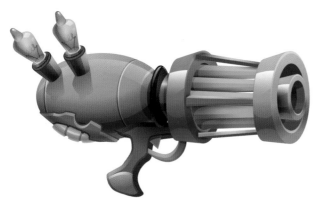

BETA
(BAY-TUH)

Noun: a version of a game that is nearly complete. It is open to a small number of users to find bugs or problems in the game before it is released. See **BUG**.

BINARY
(BYE-NUH-REE)

Noun: the language that computers use. It is made up of a series of 1s and 0s.

BOSS

Noun: a challenging enemy found at the end of a level or game who must be defeated in a boss battle for players to progress in the game or win altogether.

BATTLE ROYALE GAME

Noun: a type of game where a large number of players compete to eliminate each other until one player or team is left as the winner.

BOT

Noun: a program that is made to behave like a real person online and can interact with a system or user.

BE RIGHT BACK

BRB (Be Right Back)

Initialism: a phrase used to let other know you'll be taking a short break. This could be useful should you need to take a secret trip to the toilet.

BREAD AND BUTTER

Noun: a game or character's best go-to combos or button sequences.

BUG

Noun: an error in a piece of software that stops it from working the way that it should do.

BUNNY HOPPING

Verb: constantly jumping around to make it much more difficult for enemies to hit you.

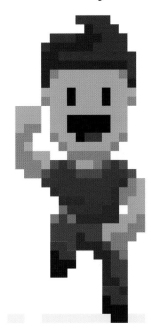

Error message

Error!

Cancel

BUTTON MASHING

Verb: a technique some people use in video games where they press as many random buttons as they can for a long period of time, in the hope that they may win.

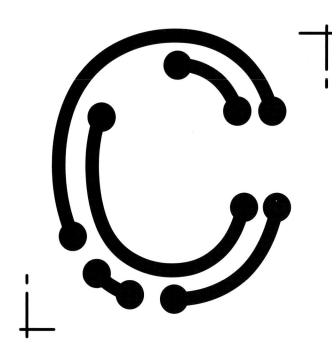

CAMERA

Noun: the angle and position from which you see what is happening in the game.

CAMPING

Verb: staying in one place, usually around a corner or in a place that is hard to spot, and shooting opponents without ever needing to move.

CGI (Computer-Generated Imagery)

Initialism: special effects used in TV, games or films, made using computers rather than video cameras.

CHEAT CODE

Noun: a special sequence of buttons used to change the normal version of the game. Some common cheats are activating extra lives or gaining extra items.

CLOUD

Noun: the large computers, called servers, that you can connect to on the internet and use for storing data, rather than using up storage on your console or device.

CODING

Verb: putting information and commands into a program to create software, apps and websites.

COMBO

Noun: a sequence of attacks that are very difficult to interrupt or block.

CONSOLE

Noun: a system dedicated to playing games.

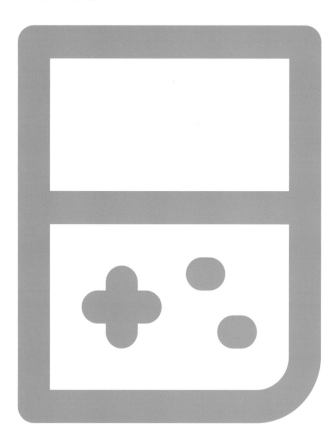

CONTROLLER

Noun: the hardware that you hold and use to direct whatever is happening on your screen.

CO-OP GAME

Noun: a type of game involving players working together in a group of two or more.

COOLDOWN

Noun: the time a player needs to wait after using a character's skill or item before it becomes available to use again.

CPU PLAYERS

Noun: characters in the game controlled by the computer. You might play against lots of these in an offline racing game.

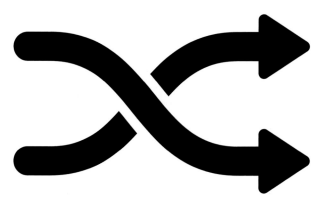

CROSS-PLATFORM GAMING

Verb: playing with or against other players online who are not on the same console as you. See **PLATFORM**.

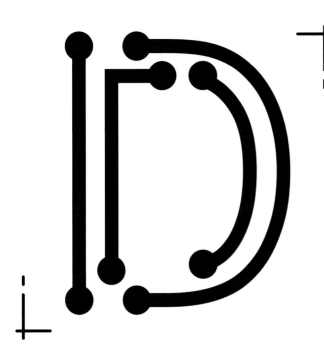

DEVS

Noun: short for developers, these are the game's creators, programmers and designers.

DLC (Downloadable Content)

Initialism: extra content for a game that can be downloaded from an online shop. This might be extra levels or new characters. Always ask a parent or guardian before getting DLC.

DEMO

Noun: a small portion of a game released by developers to give players an experience of the game before they buy it.

DOUBLE JUMP

Noun: a second jump after the first, performed by double-tapping the jump button, which lets you reach higher places.

WORD RUSH

There are a lot of words in this book, but how many of them can you make from the letters to the right in just two minutes? You can use each letter square just once for each word. Play on your own or grab a friend to challenge. Find a pen, get some paper and start the timer! 3... 2... 1...

W	T	D	G	U	I
F	D	M	L	O	P
A	E	R	T	K	C
L	K	A	U	H	B
E	A	I	N	G	U
S	M	P	O	D	K

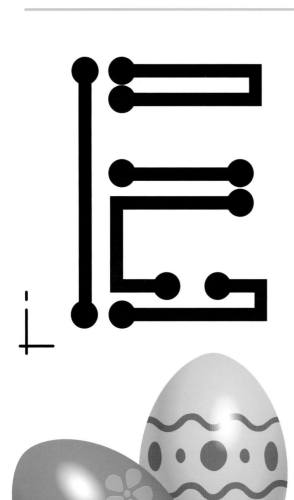

EQUIP

Verb: to take something from the game-world or your inventory and make it a useable item.

ESPORTS

Noun: multiplayer video game competitions played by professional gamers, usually for a cash prize.

EXPAND

Verb: to move out into new areas of the map in order to gather more resources.

EASTER EGG

Noun: a hidden object or feature in a game that no one is told about by the developers. There is very rarely any chocolate involved.

ENEMIES

Noun: characters that battle against the main character or try to halt their quest or journey.

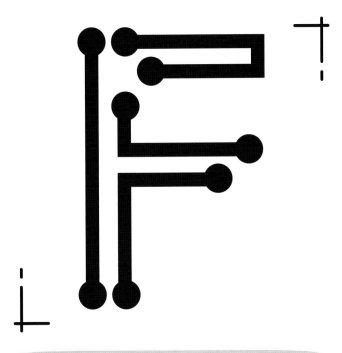

FANTASY GAME

Noun: a type of game set in a fictional universe with fictional characters, which usually has very little from real life shown in it.

FIRST-PERSON GAME

Noun: a type of game that is styled as though the player is seeing and experiencing the world themselves, through the eyes of a character.

FLAGS

Noun: items, areas or bases that must be captured by teams in multiplayer games in order to earn points or take control of a game.

FOG

Noun: an area of the map that hasn't been explored or can't be explored yet.

FRAME RATE

Noun: something used to measure how smoothly an animation moves. For example, 60 fps means that 60 frames are shown per second.

FRIENDLIES

Noun: characters or players who are either on your team or are thought of as allies.

GRAPHICS
(GRAH-FIX)
Noun: the visual images and designs produced for a game that you see on your screen.

GRAPHICS CARD
Noun: a piece of hardware inside your computer that helps the computer to display high-quality images, such as those used in games and videos.

GRUNTS
Noun: low-level enemies who are usually found in big groups but can be easily defeated.
See **ENEMIES**.

Noun: when something in a game does not work correctly, causing a problem.

GOD GAME
Noun: a game in which the player acts as an invisible god, controlling and watching a group of characters.

WORD JUMBLE

Each group of letters below is a jumbled up word from in this book. Can you rearrange the letters and figure out what each word is? If you're finding it a bit tricky, why not flick through the book to check out some of the words that might be jumbled.

1. DSEAEHT
2. GBU
3. EECOJVBIT
4. ESEMNIE

5. THLTASE
6. OCOBM
7. ELEME
8. MRAPFOLT

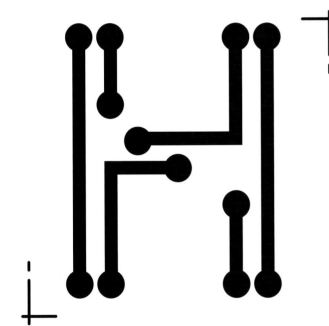

HARDWARE

Noun: physical pieces of technology, such as consoles, controllers and screens.

HD (High Definition)

Initialism: a standard of sharp image quality defined by the number of pixels across the screen. See **PIXEL**.

HDMI CABLE

Noun: a wire that connects modern games consoles to screens, capable of carrying HD and 4K data. See **HD** and **4K**.

HEADSET

Noun: a pair of headphones, usually with an attached microphone, that can be used to make the player feel like they are part of the game. See **MICROPHONE**.

#ABCDEFGHIJKLMNOPQRSTUVWXYZ

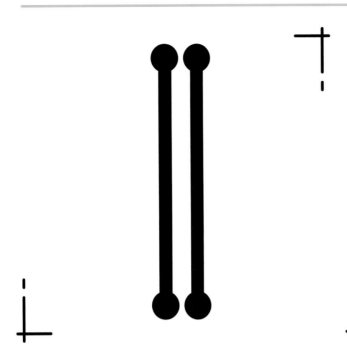

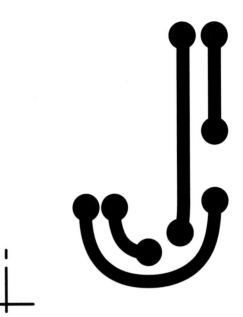

INDIE GAME (IN-DEE GAME)

Noun: a game developed by a small studio. These studios are known for being creative and taking risks.

INVENTORY

Noun: a menu of items collected by the player during the game, which can be used or equipped. See **EQUIP**.

INVISIBLE WALL

Noun: a certain point in a game-world where the character might hit a wall that can't be seen. The character can usually be seen walking pointlessly on the spot.

ITEM LEVEL

Noun: a number attached to an item, such as a weapon or armour, that shows its power.

JOYSTICK

Noun: a controller with a moveable stick, which moves or controls something in the game.

JRPG (Japanese Role-Playing Game)

Initialism: a type of RPG that originated in Japan and usually features an anime style, a type of Japanese animation. See **RPG**.

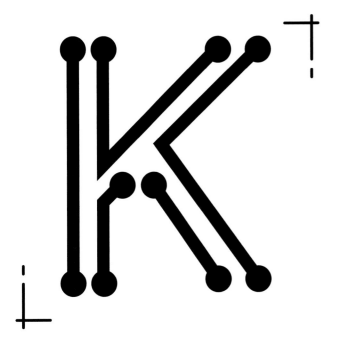

KILL-DEATH RATIO

Noun: the number of enemies you have defeated compared to the number of times your character has been defeated. The higher your ratio, the better player you are.

KEYBOARD WARRIOR
(KEE-BORD WOR-REE-UH)

Noun: someone who only has arguments online rather than in real life.

KINGMAKING

Verb: choosing which other player wins (by the way you play), when you don't believe you can win the game.

TIP: DON'T GET INTO A WAR WITH A WARRIOR.

Keyboard warriors use video game chats and private messages to make you feel angry or upset. Do not respond to messages from people like this. Turn off your console and take a break, or block the player. You should speak to an adult if someone is upsetting you online.

KNOCKDOWN

Noun: when a player is knocked to the floor and can't immediately recover. Sometimes the player who has been knocked down will need the help of another player within a limited time to recover.

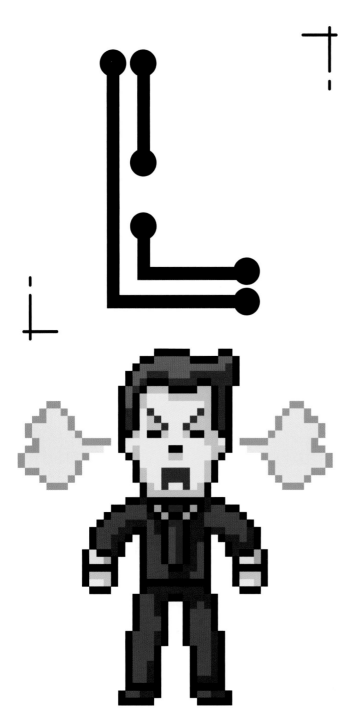

happening and get every friendly character, including yourself, killed as a result.

LET'S PLAY

Noun: a playthrough of a video game where the player provides commentary about the game as they play it. This is usually released as a series of videos for the entertainment of others.

LEVEL

Noun: a section or part of a game. Most games are broken up into different levels that must be completed one after the other.

LOOT BOX

Noun: a virtual box of rewards for completing levels or objectives. The box includes random items such as weapons and upgrades.

LAG

Noun: a delay between pressing a controller button and the action on the screen. Bad losers will often blame lag.

LEEROY JENKINS

Verb: a person's name that is shouted out if you rush into a situation without knowing what's

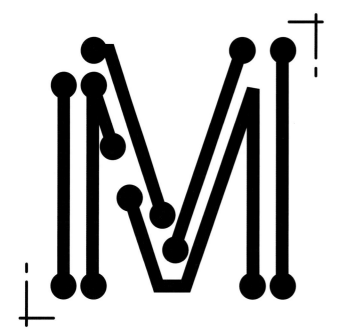

MELEE (MEH-LAY)

Adjective: a type of attack used when you are in close contact with an enemy, such as a punch or use of a handheld weapon.

MAP

Noun: a full screen or section of the screen that shows you where you are and which parts of the world are around you.

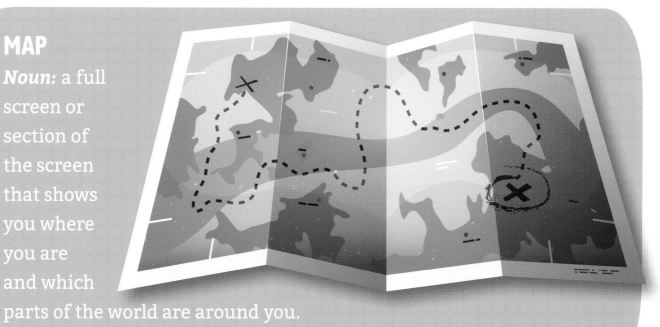

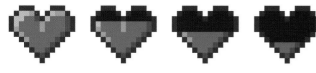

MECHANICS (MEH-KAN-IX)

Noun: the way that a game operates, such as how health, movement and combat work.

MENU

Noun: a list of options available to you. Unfortunately, there's no food to be found here.

MICROPHONE

Noun: a piece of hardware that can be spoken into and sends the sound to be played out of another player's screen or headphones.

MICROTRANSACTIONS

Noun: small payments that can be used to gain advantages over other players, or to customise a single-player experience. See **DLC**.

MMORPG (Massively Multiplayer Online Role-Playing Game)

Initialism: a type of game where lots of users can connect to the internet to play against each other. It doesn't have the catchiest of names.

MOBILE GAMING

Verb: playing a game on a portable device, such as a handheld console or a mobile phone.

MULTIPLAYER

Noun: a game mode that involves playing with or against more than one person at the same time.

MoCAP

Noun: a technique used by video game developers to help them record a real-life actor's movements and transfer them into a game. Also known as Motion Capture.

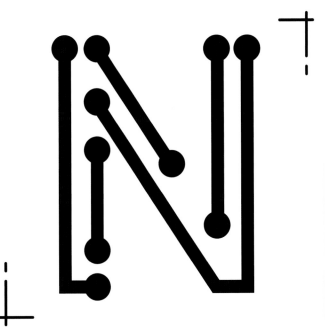

NO-SCOPE

Verb: defeating an enemy by using a sniper rifle and not even looking down the scope.

NOOB

Noun: short for newbie, a noob is a person who is new to a game and doesn't know what they're doing yet.

NERF

Verb: changing a game to weaken an object, tactic, weapon or ability in order to fairly balance a game. This is usually done by developers. See **DEVS**.

NETWORK

Noun: computers and devices that are linked together within a building or area.

NINTENDO

Noun: a Japanese games company founded in 1889. They started making video games in the 1970s and have created consoles such as the Wii and the Switch.

NPC (Non-Playable Character)

Initialism: a character, controlled by part of the game, that rarely takes part in the action.

#ABCDEFGHIJKLMNOPQRSTUVWXYZ

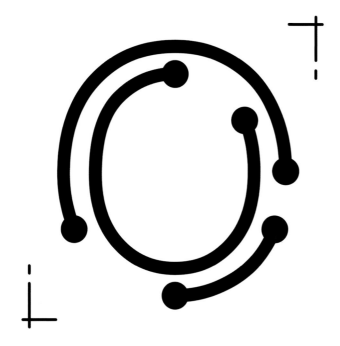

ONLINE GAMEPLAY

Noun: playing with or against other players using the internet. See **MULTIPLAYER**.

OP (Overpowered)

Initialism: when an item, weapon, ability or tactic is too powerful, making a game unfair.

OBJECTIVE

Noun: a target or goal that must be achieved to either continue or win in a single-player or multiplayer game.

ONE-SHOT

Verb: to defeat an enemy instantly. This usually requires a high level of skill... or an amazing weapon.

OPEN WORLD

Noun: a map that is fully open to be explored from the start of the game without any restrictions.

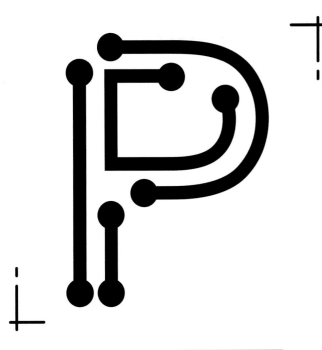

P

PEGI (Pan European Game Information)

Acronym: a rating system that tells players the age they need to be to play the game. The ratings are 3+, 7+, 12+, 16+ and 18+.

PIXEL

Noun: a tiny unit of a digital image. When you look at a picture on a computer you are looking at a collection of hundreds, thousands or even hundreds of thousands of tiny coloured dots.

PATCH

Noun: a type of update sent out by game developers to improve or fix problems in a game that has already been released.

PLATFORM

Noun: a console, computer or device that video games can be played on.

PC (Personal Computer)

Initialism: a system that games can be played on. PCs can be upgraded to deal with the most complex and detailed games.

A B C D E F G H I J K L M N O P Q R S T U V W X Y Z

PLATFORM GAME

Noun: a type of game that requires the player to jump, climb and travel across lots of platforms, usually while avoiding obstacles.

PLAYSTATION

Noun: a gaming brand owned by Sony Interactive Entertainment, created in 1994. It has created consoles such as the PS4 and PS Vita.

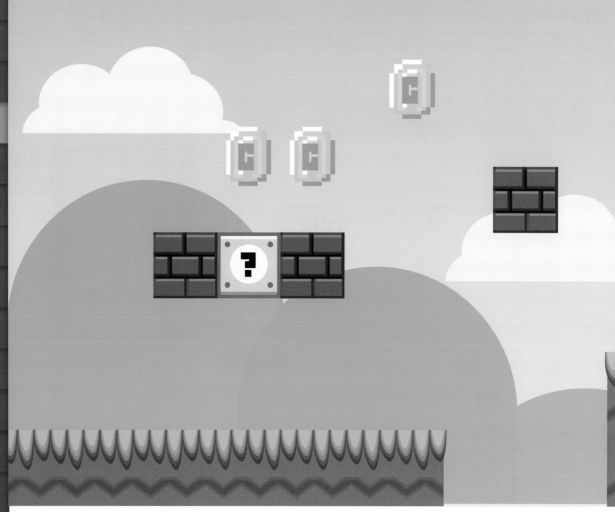

POWER-UP

Noun: an item that gives your character special abilities, usually only for a short time.

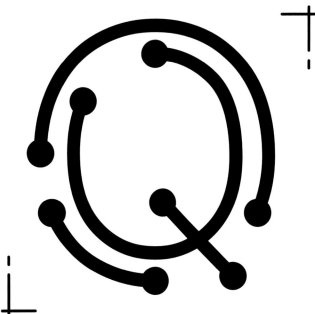

QR CODE

Noun: a square with lots of smaller square and rectangular shapes inside that can be scanned by a device and used to launch a website.

QUEST

Noun: an activity that is part of the storyline, usually with specific objectives that need to be achieved before moving on.

QUICK TIME EVENT

Noun: a sequence in a game where the player needs to perform actions on their controller very quickly when instructions appear on the screen.

QUICKSAVE

Noun: a feature that allows you to save your progress in a game at the touch of a button.

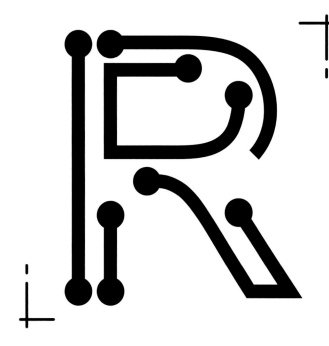

REWARDS

Noun: items, characters or levels that can be unlocked as a result of completing an achievement.

RPG (Role-Playing Game)

Initialism: a type of game where you take control of the life of a particular character.

RTS (Real-Time Strategy)

Initialism: a type of game where players must control different objects or groups in real-time to out-think other players or the computer.

RACING GAME

Noun: a type of game that places players against other players (virtual or real) to see who can drive the fastest around a track or from one point to another.

RAGE QUIT

Verb: to get so angry at a game that you quit at the end of, or during, a game.

RESPAWN

Verb: to return to the world or map after your character has died.

RETRO GAMES

Noun: classic games from a long time ago, which are still played today.

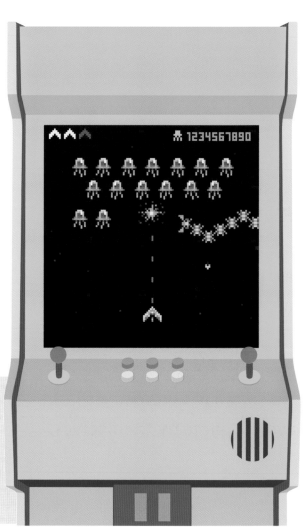

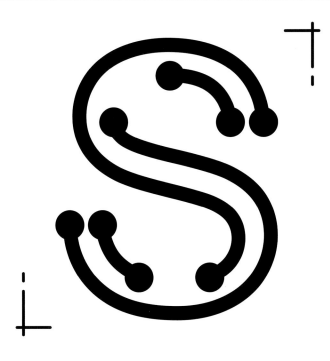

SANDBOX

Noun: an environment or game mode where you can try out anything and roam freely.

SHOOTER GAME

Noun: a type of game that gives the player a weapon which must be used to defeat all enemies.

SINGLE PLAYER

Noun: a mode where one player plays the game by themselves.

SPLIT-SCREEN

Noun: a type of multiplayer for two or more players playing together on the same screen. The screen is separated into halves or quarters, which act as separate screens.

SQUEAKER

Noun: someone who starts screaming down their microphone when they lose or die in an online game.

STEALTH

Adjective: a style of playing that involves quiet, sneaky actions which go unnoticed by enemies.

STREAMING

Verb: broadcasting the video and sound from a video game across the internet, so that other people can watch.

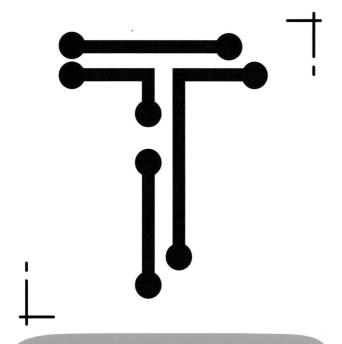

TIME TRIAL

Noun: a game mode that challenges players to complete an objective against the clock. Every second counts!

TOURNAMENT

Noun: a competition that works by either totalling points or eliminating other players in order to crown a winner.

TAKE THE L

Verb: to accept loss or failure. People might use this phrase to rub in their exceptional victory over you.

THIRD-PERSON GAME

Noun: a game that is styled as though you are controlling a visible character, usually from a camera angle above and behind them.

TREE

Noun: an interactive chart that displays a character's progression, usually unlocking skills or attributes along the way.

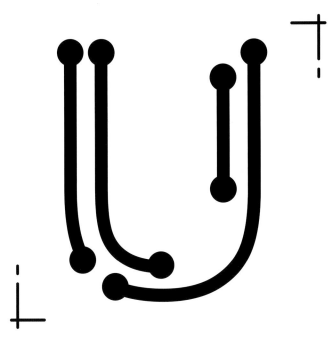

UPGRADE

Verb: a way to make an item or character even more powerful.

UPLOAD

Verb: to post something on the internet.
You should always be certain that you want something to be seen by everyone before you upload it.

UNDERPOWERED

Adjective: when an item, weapon, ability or tactic isn't powerful enough to compete against other players.

UNLOCK

Verb: to gain access to something that wasn't available before.

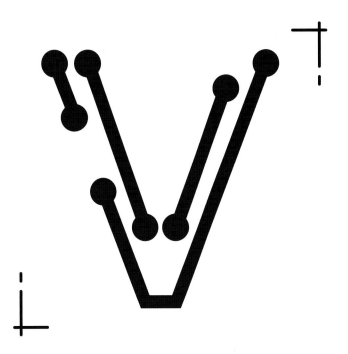

VAPOURWARE

Noun: video games that are announced and developed, but never actually get released.

VIRTUAL OBJECT

Noun: a real-life object that has been remade in a video game.

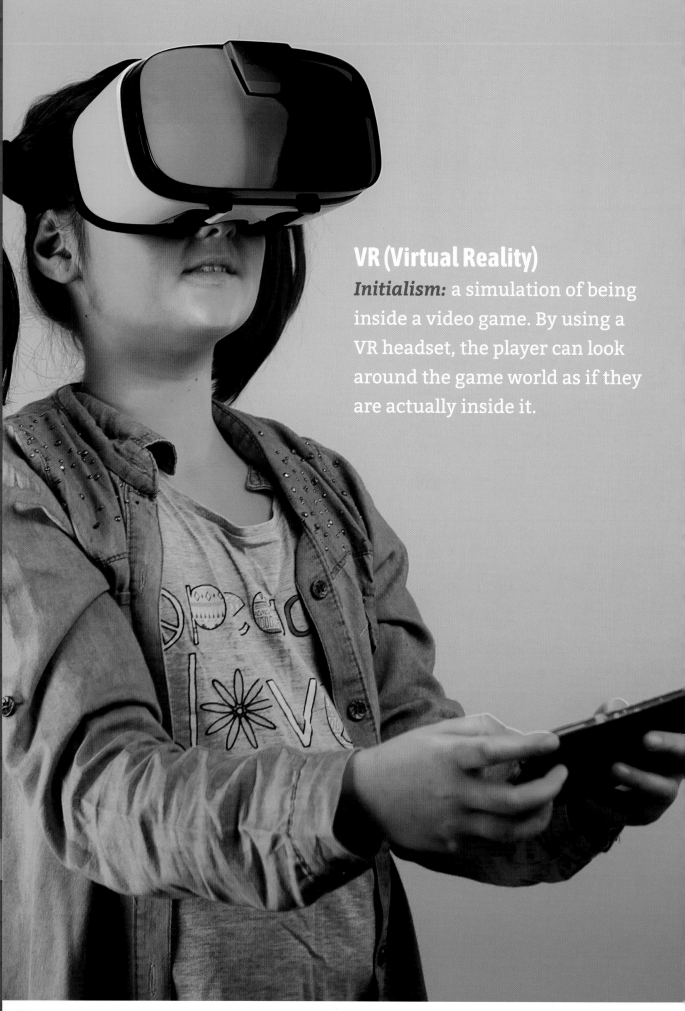

VR (Virtual Reality)

Initialism: a simulation of being inside a video game. By using a VR headset, the player can look around the game world as if they are actually inside it.

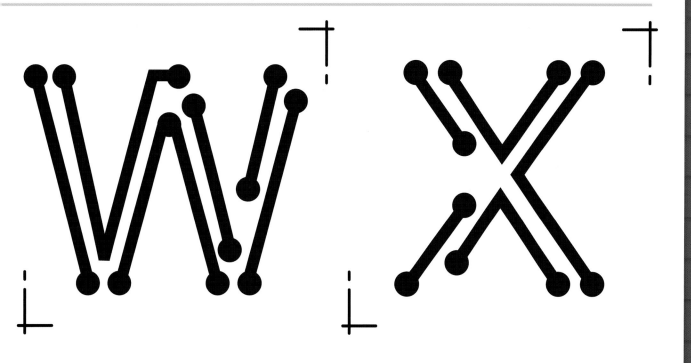

WALKTHROUGH

Noun: a written description of a game, intended to guide players through how to complete it if they're struggling to beat it.

WAVE

Noun: a round of enemies, usually increasing in numbers each time, from whom you need to defend a set point.

XBOX

Noun: a video game brand owned by Microsoft, created in 2001. It has created consoles such as the Xbox One and the Xbox 360.

XP (Experience Points)

Initialism: points that are used to show progress towards higher levels, gained by simply playing the game.

WORLD

Noun: the entire explorable area of a game. Worlds can be completely open, or have areas closed off.

WORD SEARCH

You've learned the language of video games, but can you spot some of the words in a crowd? Can you De:Code this word search and find all 15 words?

D	S	A	R	N	D	S	E	T	E	Q	U	I	P	J
U	A	H	W	A	V	E	R	V	T	R	W	S	Y	O
Y	L	M	P	E	S	Z	W	C	A	A	G	M	N	V
S	N	E	M	C	E	N	D	O	J	C	U	Q	O	R
T	X	N	B	O	G	D	E	N	W	E	C	Y	O	P
I	N	U	A	W	F	B	N	T	O	R	A	K	W	P
C	H	V	D	G	S	O	Y	R	E	W	M	U	H	O
R	E	V	B	L	A	T	J	O	Y	S	T	I	C	K
C	A	M	P	I	N	G	S	L	A	K	D	G	F	I
E	D	R	O	D	D	V	H	L	G	L	I	T	C	H
J	S	G	Y	B	B	R	S	E	G	A	M	O	T	E
M	E	S	N	O	O	B	Y	R	E	S	X	B	U	F
I	T	F	E	S	X	C	S	H	Y	E	W	L	H	G
N	D	S	R	S	Q	U	P	I	X	E	L	B	A	C
A	F	I	X	Q	P	K	T	E	X	D	T	I	J	G

AMMO	BOSS
CAMPING	CONTROLLER
EQUIP	GLITCH
HEADSET	JOYSTICK
LAG	MENU
NOOB	PIXEL
RACER	SANDBOX
WAVE	